W0017155

The Geometry
of Wishes

The Geometry
of Wishes

Randall Watson

Texas Review Press
Huntsville, Texas

FIRST EDITION

Requests for permission to acknowledge material from the work should be
sent to:

Permissions
Texas Review Press
English Department
Sam Houston State University
Huntsville, TX 77341-2146

Cover art: *Nocturne III* by Jacqueline Dee Parker

Interior art: Randall Watson

Author photo: Linda Daigle

Cover design: Nancy Parsons, www.graphicdesigngroup.net

Library of Congress Cataloging-in-Publication Data

Names: Watson, Randall, author.
Title: The geometry of wishes / Randall Watson.
Description: First edition. | Huntsville, Texas : Texas Review Press, [2018]
    | Identifiers: LCCN 2018002041 (print) | LCCN 2018003860 (ebook) | ISBN
    9781680031621 (ebook) | ISBN 9781680031614 | ISBN 9781680031614q(pbk.)
Subjects: | LCGFT: Poetry.
Classification: LCC PS3623.A873 (ebook) | LCC PS3623.A873 A6 2018 (print) |
    DDC 811/.6--dc23
LC record available at https://lccn.loc.gov/2018002041

To rivers: "for trying to convince us
they are made exclusively of light."
—*bustalk*

Contents

The Geometry
of Wishes

Teaching Myself to Read

I want to call it *autopsia*,

I want to call it *aubade*,

I want to call it *tenderness, return:*

in the flower's throat
the history of bees

I

Autumn Sonata (A Love Poem for Strangers)

I am slip and sleeve-length,
             an evening, undecided, corduroy,
         the edge of a river,
   fish net, white, dimpled water;
here is my soft, my red,
         my quick breath, morning's
hi-lites, like a boy in his limber,
   swimming, a blue curious,
         one gray shoe on the wet dock.
This is tomorrow, fleece, and teal, and trimmed
         with January, large glassed and looking
                 vociferous, interested, suddenly,
taller than dust, somewhat weekend,
         pencilled, summer, lovely, transient,
a woman in overtures,
                 that musical season.
All the startings, the forward, leaning,
   into closeness, conversation,
         the cuneiform salve
of the mouth, the runic, climactic, indecipherable,
         body and sap—our legs, loose color,
like strings, shuffled and touched,
         the redwood, spruce, vascular
course of us,
   shortwaisted, wide, leafless, whatever,
in sparkle, familiar, quartet.

Emerging into Autumn from a Nantucket Cabana

I

The sun to the east, at the edge
of the water, too bright to look at.
And the sand has a slippery feel,
like chalk beaded with silver.

There's a distant bell, maybe a ship's bell,
a church's recording. A distant bluff
cramped in shadow. Sailboats docked
at the little harbor, bobbing

in the tidal shift. A laughing gull
that isn't laughing. So much, he thinks.
So little. The ease
of a simple landscape. Its reticence,

the back and forth
of the circumscribed waters
peaking the slips,
withdrawing.

II

He can't quite recall what day it is,
one of the gifts of travel. And he

can sense a forest loneliness
though without the forest. Something

poised. Extensive. Inhabited.
With excellent posture.

III

But he is waiting for her to change,
and for a moment, he is possessed
by the waiting. His bare
legs grow cold. His left knee

aches. A brown line of seaweed
bristles with flies, resurrected
by the light and coming heat.
The sky makes for flat and shallow,

pressing, slow. But when she emerges
pushing the canvas flap aside,
her dark arm extending from the dark,
it's an immeasurable passage—

her pastel one-piece,
her beautiful history
of giving and taking, the shoreline's
instant numerous, serious

with morning. Not severe, but the way
a mysterious, interior joy
can be serious, how she appears
with all that water around her.

IV

Let's call this the whatevertime,
the daybreak impulse—

cool enough to admire her breath
make that measure appear

where all things are a sounding.

Once Grief Has Entered

A pulse, you said.

Liminal. Braided.

As in that maple where the meadow lifts,
its full crown like the halo of a flare,
a mean of interbranching light
in a floating share of brown and green,
luminescent, motional.

Or that autumn outside Albany
when the trees opened
and the pond emerged
from the scratchy shadows
bright as resin.

Strange, isn't it, what sometimes hurts us.

The heron, blue and great and passing far above,
so slow and graceful it is not flight
but the sheer gentleness of air,
as it eases its way down to the willows.

How it arches its wings
and lifts for a moment,
almost weightless,
before it touches down.

II

Trailways, August 28, 1963

We crossed the exhilarating, high-pitched.
Passed the stench and glittering,
the amusement bright, the gradual,
box apartments by the tracks and stations
squatting like bored and patient orphans
waiting for a Sunday market to begin.

Then the green-bordered interstates.

Hay-bales scattered like formalist sculptures, cornfields
with their stiff stalks and rag-doll tassels
limp as puppets hung
in a storage closet.
Side woods snarled with briar and ivy.
Oaks and maples.

Then rummy and old maid
at the little table rearward and nearby
the cramped bathrooms
that stank of chemicals and soap and piss
splattered on the metal floor, flecks
of snow-white shaving foam
clinging to the shadowy mirror.

Racks of bags and suitcases and light jackets
dreaming above our heads
like hibernating mammals.

The chrome bright
burnings of the little towns,

those signs for *Burma Shave* and *Stuckeys* and
The World's Largest Rabbit
and men in large hats and fringed buckskin
wearing side-arms on the porch
of a mock saloon.

Birds scrolling the staves of the infrastructure.

Men outside a church
brushing ashes from their sleeves.

Wives and daughters and mothers touching their hair
as if to measure themselves,

waving little paper fans
stapled to paint-sticks
where Jesus kneels, alone
in the midst of his drowsy, sleeping disciples,
knowing the story his body will tell.

And then my grandfather
sitting on the back stoop with his .22
shooting sparrows, which dirty the sidewalk.

Dust blowing off the fields.

Small purple flowers
speckled with dew and foraging ants.

He's dipping bread in a cup of milk, disregarding
the plate of tomatoes, red as transitions.

Crushing his Pall Mall in the drive.

Pulling two hot 7Ups from the trunk
of his Oldsmobile.

And those boys
in jeans-jackets who gather
outside *Peguy's*,
the only women's clothing store in town,
car hoods raised, adjusting
the air intake or idle, gunning
the engine.

Wiping the oil-stick clean
with a slash of newsprint.

Attuned to the mechanical contrivance.

Discovering their blurred faces in the polished armature.

There near the geographical
heart of the country.

38 North by 97 West.

Entranced by the sheen.

Great Plains Pastoral

The equipment was large and painted brightly.

And the fields went on and were sometimes fallow and bare,

and sometimes men gathered by the wheezing, sputtering combine,

a tin cup dangling from an outdoor spigot by the drive.

A great horned owl lounged at dusk,

                in the dead elm by the culvert.

A doe knelt in lightning and the dark that follows.

And I was thinking about her there, vigilant, still,

                        the sky cackling and booming,

when the men who drove up in the storm and hurried

      removed their boots at the door

and my aunt said

      must have been an angel warned Verne the bridge was flooded

and someone else said

      it was just his headlights on water

and my Aunt replied—

      like the time the old plow fell from the jacks but did not pin him.

Then my cousin, Bobby, said

      luck was not a spirit of intention,

and my Uncle Wes said

      vigilance was not a habit of man

and then the power went out and the kitchen darkened.

Soon someone rummaged a candle from a drawer and burned it

and we sat there in the big shadow it made.

Forget all that nonsense about a circle of light, someone muttered.

And though our faces were shrouded

we could see our hands on the table.

Ghost Month

As if the others weren't also.

As if the moon, assuming a particular disposition, a certain aptitude,

      were the only measure.

As when the crabs, bloated with life, quicken their way to the beach-height,

that bed of split-straw and seaweed,

       to dig and scrawl,

          beyond the day's warmth,

to the dark-wet depository

         their instinct demands.

As if March were a breathing mouth and not a lamp

         baring the way upward.

Or August browning nonetheless under the early rains.

For you, we say, this bowl of basil,

champagne grapes upon their scaffold,

this white crane creased by the earnest.

What is it you seek but wonderment and delicious trouble?

That wooden stool with its finish worn bare?

The light that responds to the sound of our voices?

Take this house we burn it for you.

Can you see your grandson in the door?

The car with its wheels

      turned toward the curb to stop it from rolling?

Do not be saddened by the sudden decline of the pocket harmonica.

By the speed-wash setting on the digital machine.

Take joy in the smoke the world smoke it rises.

The night-market with its oils and cutlets.

Know that you are our recurring occasion.

That this is the expression of your coming.

That we have dug a hole and filled it

with sawdust and pitch

and set it afire and called it our longing.

That we have made ourselves into earthlight and season.

That we carry you forward into our changing,

and shall keep so till our wide-time is done.

III

Shikoku Triptych

I
Geisha Love Concerto

Woman of waters,
bodhisattva dressed in salt and mirrors,
     arms crossed and folded,
the thousand hands of evening greet you,
         fire sister, groomed by moonlight,
a prayer on the soft, wet underside
          of your upper lip:

O daughter of thread,
O shelf of jam glasses and plums,
widow of bells, of barn swallows indigo,
small mouthed also.
Palace of fishes. Youth.
Not the drop of water that falls
but the one that is rising, the one that returns
the blackeyed praise of roundness,
the frill and scallop of the mouth as it sings,
    low tide open.

Praise this brokenness.
Praise this bead and harp,
    this coldness,
white-haired evening with
      its mallet and pipe and music,
        left arm high,
the face reflected in the courtyard well
     that is luck and tomorrow,
house of muscle and breath and violin.
Give us this day.
This polished eye, this hope, this love
straightening our hair at twilight by the glare of red lanterns,
the thrill of paper
     set aflame.

II
Her Dark Mouth

I am driving. Driving to escape death,
death with its head down on my kitchen table,
death the engine, death the trunk,
death like a girl with her hair divided.

Death, I am crazed by it,
for it is hopeless,
he accompanies me always, dark bird
in the bougainvilla, yellow tail,

shooting pool at the Riverside Grill with his boney girlfriend,
        running the table.

Death who is handsome,

painting his teeth black to prevent decay,

Death with his white chalk and sponge and his love of stone,

Death the decorator—the slim giver:

This is the narrow body, he says, The thin breath,
they sustain me:

famously recalled in the works of Breughel who is dead now—
a solitary crow upon a scaffold, and if I remember correctly,
a world covered in snow and more snow, space and more space,
death's welcome, death's emptiness, death's gift,

which is what I run from in my quick cart, four wheels
        driving madly west,
though I know it is hopeless,

hoping nonetheless my hopelessness
        might save me.

West—where death is a white beach,
a tired woman napping on her towel, topless,
because she wants someone to touch her even as she sleeps,
to feel, like death, the heat and softness of her skin,
to find, like a blind man turning toward her,
her dark mouth.

III
Rest Now, Sleep

I have been to the temple of weaving and cutting,
Water racing at the edge of the rice fields.
And to the temple of the great sun, also,
By the temple of Burning Mountain,
One of the bright places of the earth,
Light like a long welcome among the cedars.

Here is warmth and shadow.
Here is the turning to go when the going has come,
Taking the ten nights with you,
One white stone hidden in the hand, wisteria blooming.

Thus one's father is there, in the turning,
And one's children, too, like a well that has been tasted,
And the women you have loved in their sandals of cloth,
Their feet painted turquoise,
Their hair as black and dark as a room to rest in
When you cannot bear the burden of sight,
Your spirit thin and long beside the blue slenderness of their bodies.

Rest now, sleep. The body and its braille of departure.
Like the crane whose body is its form of speech
And what it says it says by standing in water.

The Dakini (1)

Rest, she says. And listen.

It is as though the sea were a place that was made to sleep near, I say,
a dark girl whose darker nipples make new secrets for the mouth.

But there are no secrets in the mouth, she says,
because the mouth, even shut against itself, is always sung and open.

Maybe that is its secret, I'd like to reply,
but I am filled, suddenly, with the instrument of her voice,

and I can hear it,
the hot sand, the water, the coming sleep

and its welcome.

The Dakini (2)

No death, she says. No dying.
Sometimes the white dog sleeps in the sun.
The clover rises up above the grass to welcome the brightness.
A footstool rusts on an office roof.
Only what lasts is real, she says, and you can find it.
Not in the thing itself but in the place it comes from.
The sky like the roof of a cave the horses cross under.
The speckled bird and its circling analogies.
The eye as large as everything it sees,
and the generous and empty mind it rests in.
No work but in the watching.
No labor but in the letting go.
All the beauty between the stillness and the changing.

Treasure

Tiger's Eye. Apache Tear.
A crushed napkin from the Black Eyed Pea
where Valerie left me.
A small wooden Maitreya
the so-called 'happy' Buddha
of the future
missing a foot.
A bit of broken scrimshaw
from Alaska.

And here,
a two ball from Lola's
that graffiti bar where the women dressed
in teddies and Maori tattoos.

And a picture of Alice
you remember Alice
a bartender there
whose lips seemed perpetually swollen
as though she spent her afternoons bruising them
ever so slightly
with the chilled smooth curve
of the common water glass.

I can imagine her, even now,
sitting at her kitchen table,
the brittle antique formica
edged by steel,
a poster of Mick Jagger on the fridge,
baring her teeth as her lips parted,
welcoming the round clear pressure
she brought against herself
to make herself pretty.

Dear Alice

When hats hat hats are hatted,
When rabbits rabbit it's rabbits.
When worms worm it's worms come out
The little fellows.

But when hats don't hat no hats are hatted,
The bald head shines in the rain.
And when rabbits don't rabbit, then
rabbits won't jump again.
And when worms don't worm and
No worms come

The hats will rabbit and the rabbits will worm.
And the worms won't squiggle
And the rabbits won't hide
And the hats will be empty inside.

Nostalgia

Elbowed from the fastness on a court in Brooklyn

I named it *Regatta,*

I called it *Ruin,*

I signed it *Amalgam Tattoo*—

My tooth angling backwards towards the throat,

Peering into the twilight of the mouth:

A cockatiel, all unborn white,

In search of a peanut.

v

The Recital

I am older now, still with that hint of disbelief that accompanies—
particularly in a world that favors youthfulness with such vigor—
the changes that an unmarried girl cannot find within her face
the morning after her first intercourse. And yet, strangely,
what disturbs me—evenings when I am stuck in traffic and the snow
is falling and some moment rises, intense and burning and without irony,
and I am amazed at its freshness still inside me—what disturbs me
is not my age but the uncanny sense that what I thought was mine,
the things within my life that I believe in and have chosen,
are not my own at all, but merely the expression of
those conventions through which—by the habit of a man's thought
that finds comfort in believing what others believe—
I might rest secure in the mirror of the world.

Of course I do not, cannot, sincerely believe this. But nonetheless,
it is with this feeling, this sense of the unrecognizable
within my present self, that I recall a girl whose memory holds,
as though an end to wakefulness, a primacy which antedates
my years of work and love and places them, somehow, beyond me,
like a tree on a hill or a house in a field of grass, panoramic,
if you will, so faraway and unfamiliar.

Regardless, then, let me say it was summer. The early
summer of a hundred years ago—robins dropping
like gliders onto the new grass, a blackbird rustling about
in the depths of the blossoming lilac: that good part
of a person's youth that comes before one knows enough
to know themselves, and one is as entranced by some small shattering
of glass glittering upon the apex of the street
as the racing whitewash of the sea. It was the summer
of the piano, or to be even more specific, June, the month of recitals,
or for me, the month of, not love, but that mysterious excitement
we confuse it with.

I had seen her before, this girl. She lived but two blocks
south of my own, on the same street, and though this was not far,

her house was located in one of those inexplicable geographies
that strike a child as being from another world—
not because of the distance itself, but because
while two blocks east or west were friends' houses
and parks that from repeated visits had become
as familiar and as present as my own backyard, all things
north and south existed in that far and awkward terrain
that was as foreign and as strange to me as an unexplored continent.

Whether or not this 'exoticism' (that benign face of otherness)
contributed to my eventual though sudden sense of her
I do not know, nor, I think, could I hope to. Such distances,
I suspect, as we pretend to have from the intimate nature
of our encounters, are themselves rooted in
our individual lives and thus impelled
by their own proximities, where each ensuing clarification possesses,
like a matryoshka doll of Boris Yeltsin which, when opened,
progresses through a legacy of asiatic potentates
to culminate upon a tiny Lenin, its own personal and thus
particular and despotic character.

It is true, of course, I had seen her before, annually at least, I think,
occasionally, if our lessons were, by some accident, scheduled sequentially.
And it is also true that I had noticed her—or in other words my head
        had, figuratively, turned,
there was a pause within me as though the thoughts that surged
perpetually through my mind had for a moment stopped and settled there,
opinionless, upon the presence of her, her face and hair, and I felt
that sense of quiet we describe when we are curiously struck, by a
        vision, say,
and open to the striking.

But even this, clarified by retrospect, preceded the moment,
the unsayable thing that happened later. For months
she was to me a kind of shadow, or more accurately, a change
in the quality of light at my periphery, as like the quickness of a bird
that repeatedly sweeps past the edges of one's vision,
or as when our own dim interests make, unwittingly,

a fastness of ourselves to witness back to us, a geometry,
so to speak, of wishes.

It was not until the recital itself that she became to me
what now I can only vaguely remember, not as an image
but an event that plays through me still, like the wings
of a sparrow as it hovers momentarily above
the limb of the dogwood it will land upon. It was there—
outside and after the music and applause had almost faded,
and the part of the body that had withheld its blood or breath
in anticipation of the performance had unclenched itself.
It was then—there among the grass and street and brightness of the day—
that she became all slenderness to me, and tallness,
with the quickness of an uprisen light. It was as though
I had been struck by a form of blindness that excluded
all things but the thin and towering suddenness of her,
and upon which all other weights and shapes must rest.
How can I put it but to say that she was beautiful to me then—
all bone and straight hair, long-armed and smiling. Musically,
it was as though the thumb of her right hand had swung
beneath her fingers to complete a scale—like a swan that pauses
to preen beneath a wing. Or that, if one were to watch
her hands as she played, one might notice how her knuckles
rolled and scalloped like only the surface of a water can
that has been suggested by the wind. This, at least, was the feel of it,
like that wildness we encounter in ourselves when we find, abruptly
and with the kind of violence one might associate with rivers in the spring,
another person, unnamed and vital and strangely
present, before us.

This, perhaps, is why I recall her now. It must be. And while
I do not understand, not as some explicable concretion,
I know, inside myself, the purpose of her arrival—even then—
that now, older, alone, the upward surge of her in my memory and heart
is as a resurrection—like a light that startles and leaps beyond
the part of me that holds to youth and age and flesh as endings—
and gives to me this day through which the sun progresses,
bright and overhead and full of praise.

VI

Xalapa

For a month, now, I have been walking the city.

I like the way the girls rest their hands on their boyfriends' shoulders
to adjust a shoe.

The way a man bends over, back to the wind, to light a cigar.

How the gypsy women roam the park in their long dresses seeking
 donations.

Their faded brochures. The boys in fandango outside the cathedral.

And the smell of grease and oil at the little garage

is familiar and comforting. The chime of a ratchet or wrench

dropped in a toolbox. The graceful and threatening

loops of razor wire

coiling the wall-tops. Glass and mortar. Rebar

piercing the unfinished columns of houses.

Prayer flags of drying laundry. Lace and cotton.

Sometimes I walk long, far

from the city center. Doors

slanting like a blade. Little braziers

glowing in the shallow interiors. Glassed candles

barring the windows. A lisping kettle.

But at my little house I can burn a fire too. I can hang

my jacket from the canisters of gas

that lean against the kitchen wall. Green steel.

The color of caribbean sand. Sunday's trumpeter

ascending the *callé*, waking the roosters.

Sometimes Maliyel, my friend, invites me over

for camel straights and espresso. *Socorro*, she tells me,

is not some kind of wind, but one

of the names of sadness. Things

we are strong for. Assistance. Succor.

Then her son, Galo, calls down

from his sleeping loft, Randáll, *buenas dias!*

Last night, at the *Téatro, Endgame.*

Capacity, eighty-five.

A cluster of pins

stuck in a wooden table

shining in a desk lamp's half-dollar

halogen brightness. All mauve at the margins,

like a nineteenth century curtain.

Maliyel wondered if metaphor revealed a unity

hidden in the shape of things. What Paz conjectured,

though he's dead now, of course.

Sun and stone. Speckles of quartz in a granite outcrop.

So this morning Galo and I play soccer.

I call it soccer because I live in Houston.

Maliyel comes out to watch, and is smiling.

He moves the ball between his feet, delicate,

precise, easing it with the outside of his foot

before he shoots. And we welcome it as it enters

into the air. There is nothing to protect. Nothing

to save. It is quite beautiful as it rises.

Refugee

Put your loudness to rest   she says

the slender that changes
the fat brightness travelling . . .

What is God but a tree
and we, bark
peeling from the trunk . . .

Betrayed by the mouth   betrayed by the eye . . .

This is what the world does to our love of it . . .

crushing a dried cricket with her thumb . . .

And then she laughs

a rustle of paper to startle the flying things
which flee.

Mitla

To say yes and yet
know nothing—

                  like a swing
that rattles and grows still.

Such dependencies.
Such ruin.

The pinecone's clenched petals
curling open,

the faces of the passengers
on the tour bus
                    tethered
to wind and dust.

Is everything
compelled toward vacancy?

Even that fat monk
grunting up the steep hill,
that cold bee clinging
to his gray collar?

VII

Laurels from India (Oaxaca)

It's ten before noon. The bells ring
as if announcing the heat, the day
like a boy with his wooden fan
who whines from the shadows.

One woman chooses the brightness,
a chair in the sun, the sweat
pouring from her, the light on her back
and neck and hair,

while the bells, urgent, long, diachronic,
like the shallow, translucent edge of a river
at its uncut, eddying bank,
curl back upon themselves

in a swirl of self-return, their slow
persistent, offshore center
as deep and cool as a kind of winter—
all that water sounded against itself,

the part that it can carry, measured
in its depth, fish and mountain—

ice and shells and the bones
of small birds. At last, as a crowd gathers,

the heat assumes its familiar form,
accumulates into a fullness,
a perpetual hovering, like a dragonfly
tattooed on a white girl's upper arm,

am image of half-sleep and drowse,
the ancient epoch of a dream
drawn on the body. Soon,
a band starts up. Brass,

the cathedral behind it, musicians almost
leaning against the cool stone as they play,
the song like a small French circus
with a limber girl spinning in air.

They say they are going to cut
the laurels down, those gentle centuries,
there where Eisenstein and Lowry sat
in shadow, the green night at the height

of going. Each spring the jacaranda
bloom, a violet haze upon the land,
the framboyan like an orange
umbrella, the bright gown

of a sad virgin. But next year, too
soon, with its hermetic, umbilical knot,
you can't imagine it—undone—
the great trees uprooted.

Television

You need it this other life.
You need its leotard and muscle its bang
And smatter its preening detective.
You need its triplicate its nurse.
You need its special.

What would the darkness be without its invisible accent without
its register its pipe its current its goof its liquid and crystal
    its ridge of white feathers.

What you want is exclusion is wardrobe emergency.
Is tryst and purse the fat scent of lilacs
stomp and patter.

All day long you do what you do
Not want to get
What you need.

And what you need is this:
cartoon and vampire and virus travel. Catch and repair.
The hectic report of malevolent weather.

Spanish Cairns

First one, alone in the grass,
hidden like a quail's egg

to mark the place they dumped
the body. Then two,

then three, then four, a clutch,
a ring, a covey, a stack, a henge,

a pyramid of stone,
body on body.

Perhaps that boy, handing out pamphlets.
Perhaps that tailor, his fingers

streaked with chalk,
who measured the general's inseam.

Soon a growing pile of stones
at the edge of a wood

on the rise of a hill
in the shadow of lindens.

A century of stones.

A circle of stones
where the two hands meet.

A parenthetical.

The thin attorney who never married.
The government clerk who stamped your passport.

VIII

Anatomy of Melancholy

I. Furies

She bought the fastest of horses.

Saddled him and slipped
the silver bit between his teeth,

raced northward through the late October,
the saddlebags of oats and guilders

jangling beside her. For three days
she hurried through the falling snow,

past the camps of Gustavus Adolphus,
the billets of the Imperial Army,

then stopped beside a frozen pond,

the ice as thin and white as scrawls of chalk.

Kneeling there, she broke the surface
with an elbow and a hank of shale,

and when she reached in deep
below the clotted slush

to ladle the cold water up,
she saw a minnow swirling in her palm,

a speck of light she took into her mouth and swallowed.

What a strange joy that was,
the cold and cleanness of the water

falling through her,
how it settled and filled

the vague space inside she'd never measured,
a world, she imagined, where the fish

in its quick glittering,
even there in the dark bottom,

could wander.

II.   Night

Night is holiday. Is sister early. Wrapping and surprise.

Like these athletic carnations

pinned to my shirt:
a wonderland pharmacy.

Sometimes I look at the clouds and I am full of that reaching,

beyond that charity,

a man pursued into a ritual of color,

an obscurantist.

Once I saw a picture of a cockatiel

                              upon a one-eyed dancer's shoulder,

bright as the lamp he carried with him,

                              a perfect speck of blindness and vision.

Remember, how I showed you, there beside the pond,

                              beneath the corrugations, the blue

underwater glow, late evening,

                              the silk swaying above us,

the tint of my way forward?

Poetry, you said, when you were smooth as endless,

                                   unimprovable summer,

and I was shiny as the inside of a shell turned outwards

for everyone to see.

III.   Cortege

They drove through dust
The wind had lifted up,
Two limousines, three
Cars white and one
The color of unpolished bronze
hazed by the ungathered east,
the sun as pale as an egg in shadow.
It was as though
Not one soft, unloosened thing
Held earthward still,
Such was the force of it—
seed husks, chaff, small birds,
flecks of rusted steel, the brittle
hollows of the weeds,
scraps of bleached-out cardboard—
all was adrift: the woman, adjusting
her black rayon shift, brushing,
with the hard, flat face of her hand,
some indiscernible speck
from her favorite jacket:
the girl, unyielding, quiet,
glancing, just a little,
at the limo-driver's grip—
his soft, easy hold on the slick,
shining wheel, guiding
the long, heavy car
with its black polished armature
slowly forward, easing it
out and out and away and toward
and into its turning.

The Ukrainian Postmaster's Spring Flowers

Pert and filigreed, alert,
exuberant as undergraduates

on a beach in April . . .
that is the blossom's part,

praised and futureless,
a density of light and water.

And then a little shiver racing through
a streak in the body—

the bees, swarm upon swarm,
ransack the brightness.

This is the bitter part.
The diligent thieves.

Economical alchemists.
Their small baskets stuffed

with bank-drafts and silver,
building the hive.

As To The Tangerine

What opened
must have closed
around the light
it fed on.

And the light, somehow,
must have multiplied within
as the fruit, incremental, swelled
toward its own undoing.

Ripeness is like that.

It is how the world deceives us.

What I consume
is an interruption.

What I reap
is brightness,
unsevered, sweet.

IX

Transcompassion

If energy, undying, simply transforms.

If we all become, at some point, everything else.

If you, for instance, return as me, as part of me,

or the tangerine returns as a savant playing the oboe,

or the financier returns as a panda

which returns as a Lutheran minister

who returns as a topless dancer

who returns as a corpseflower

which returns as a man

who returns as the shadow of a man wandering the Sahara . . .

Buddhists believe you were once my mother.

You are so beautiful.

Strung out on crack at the men's center.

Evaluating the strength of the counter insurgents.

They believe that I was your mother too.

That we were both the Buddha's mother,

that we've been the mother of Jesus and his mother Mary

and the mother of Moses and Mohammed and of Siva.

And we've been his children too. And his wife Parvati.

We've been mountains like Kailash, Annapurna, Crestone Peak.

And valleys, and the grasses of valleys,

valleys with and without a supply of water.

And the mountains and valleys have been us as well,

the high points and low points,

have been our mothers.

The cobras and maggots and stink bugs

have all been our mothers.

And we have been their mothers.

Suckling the black fly, the green fly, the Japanese beetle.

Offering our arms up to ticks, crab lice, mosquitos, the famished fruit bat.

Who were all once our mothers.

Who were all once our children.

Who will be our mothers again.

Who feed on our blood to bear us back to the world.

And so.

The Sabbath

It is not a day, really.
Nor is it rest.

It is more like a decision.
The mind chooses not to do
        what it does when it is working.

If there is effort in it
        then it's not
                exactly what it claims to be,

but an energy anterior
                    to its reception,
             for those who know propose
it's not antithesis
             but welcome.

I, who do not practice it,
               must ask,
what would it mean to practice welcome,

             to be inhabited, open
from one long coming of the dark
to another?

Could I be the object
             of attention,

surrounded by the sky and the air and the light and being,

a welcome of the dust and wind and white gardenia,
a place of expulsions and sorrows, joy?

I can hardly imagine it,
the nothingness I might become,
             the whole creation somehow calm
with all its brightness coming on.

The Divers

Swimming pool. Bayou. Gulf.

                    Only the surface

changes.

              And everything we touch

is a surface. Even

                  your body, submerged,

is a surfacing.

            Simply

                to touch it proves

you have risen,

            just as I,

              being touched,

become the surface,

              too, of something.

                        Just so

do we measure

            the body, call it

                    circumference, travel,

though no one

              really knows what is

surrounded there.

           If you want you

can name it—

           whatever you wish.

Names, also,

        are a surfacing.

There is nothing good or bad

              in the surface,

only in the way we

          touch it.

            So reach

deep, love, into the wish

             of that naming

and surface

        into me. Touch

my wrist.

     Give me

       your word.

Acknowledgments

Chatauqua Review: "The Sabbath"
Chelsea: "Shikoku Triptych" "The Dakini (1)" "The Dakini (2)"
Confrontation: "Autumn Sonata"
Criterion Review: "The Ukrainian Postmaster's Spring Flowers"
Cutthroat: "Spanish Cairns"
Far Out: Poems of the 60's: "Trailways, August 28, 1963"
Goodbye Mexico: "Xalapa" "Laurels from India"
Improbable Worlds: "Transcompassion"
Literál: "Treasure" "Television"
North American Review: "Night"
Portland Review: "As To The Tangerine"
Southern Poetry Anthology VIII: Texas: "Once Grief Has Entered"
Tampa Review: "Ghost Month"

Also, very special thanks to Dave Parsons, Adam Zagajewski, and Antonio Saborit. To my editor, Kim Davis. To my colleagues and friends, Alan Ainsworth, Robert Lunday, Cliff Hudder, Syble Davis, and Sharon Klander. To A.K. and Dudley, without whom, who knows. To Trish and Leslie and Marc and Fei and Richard and Maliyel and Galo and Jian Ying, and you all know why. To Jacquie, for her lovely work and years of friendship. To the editors of the Blue Lynx Poetry Prize, the Juniper Prize, and the Tampa Review Poetry Prize, for their encouragement. Always, to my family, with love.

photo by Linda Daigle

Randall Watson's first book, *Las Delaciones del Sueño*, was published in a bi-lingual edition by the Universidad Veracruzana in Xalapa, Mexico. His *The Sleep Accusations* received the Blue Lynx Poetry Award and his novella, *Petals*, (as Ellis Reece), won the Quarterly West Novella Contest. He is also the editor of *The Weight of Addition, An Anthology of Texas Poetry* published by Mutabilis Press.

CPSIA information can be obtained
at www.ICGtesting.com
Printed in the USA
FFOW03n1643170218
45108685-45553FF

9 781680 031614